The Colours We Eat

Food ABC

Patricia Whitehouse

Raintree

www.raintreepublishers.co.uk
Visit our website to find out more information about **Raintree** books.

To order:
☎ Phone 44 (0) 1865 888112
▤ Send a fax to 44 (0) 1865 314091
▢ Visit the Raintree Bookshop at **www.raintreepublishers.co.uk** to browse our catalogue and order online.

First published in Great Britain by Raintree,
Halley Court, Jordan Hill, Oxford OX2 8EJ,
part of Harcourt Education.
Raintree is a registered trademark of Harcourt
Education Ltd.

Editorial: Nick Hunter and Diyan Leake
Design: Sue Emerson (HL-US) and Joanna Sapwell
(www.tipani.co.uk)
Picture Research: Amor Montes de Oca (HL-US)
and Maria Joannou
Production: Jonathan Smith

Originated by Dot Gradations
Printed and bound in China by South China
Printing Company

ISBN 1 844 21609 8
07 06 05 04 03
10 9 8 7 6 5 4 3 2 1

British Library Cataloguing in Publication Data
Whitehouse, Patricia
Food ABC
641.3
A full catalogue record for this book is available
from the British Library.

Acknowledgements
The publishers would like to thank the following
for permission to reproduce photographs: Amor
Monte de Oca p. 3, back cover (avocado); Anthony
Blake Photo Library p. 21 (Joy Skipper); Color Pic,
Inc. p. 23 (seed, E. R. Degginger); Craig
Mitchelldyer Photography p. 15; Dwight Kuhn
pp. 10, 21; E. R. Degginger p. 11; Gareth Boden
pp. 14, 23 (pastry, quiche); Heinemann Library
(Michael Brosilow) pp. 6, 8, 9, 16, 17, 20, 22, 23
(honey, jam, salad), back cover (ice cream); Rick
Wetherbee pp. 4, 5, 7, 19, 23 (fruit, vegetable);
Visuals Unlimited pp. 12B (Jerome Wexler), 13
(John D. Cunningham), 18 (Wally Ebert), 23
(stone, Jerome Wexler); Winston Fraser p. 12T.

Cover photograph of apple, broccoli and coconut,
reproduced with permission of Photodisc

Every effort has been made to contact copyright
holders of any material reproduced in this book.
Any omissions will be rectified in subsequent
printings if notice is given to the publishers.

 CAUTION: Children should be supervised by an adult when handling food and kitchen utensils.

Some words are shown in bold, **like this.** You can find them in the glossary on page 23.

Aa   avocado
Bb   brown

stone

Avocados have a large brown seed called a **stone** inside.

Cc colour
Dd dinner

There are lots of colours in the food in this dinner.

Ee   eat

We eat lots of different kinds of vegetables.

Ff   fruit

Honeydew melon is a
green **fruit**.

Gg green

Grapes are green fruit.

Hh honey
Ii ice cream

Honey is yellow and sticky.

This ice cream has honey on top!

Jj jam

Strawberry **jam** tastes good on bread!

Kk   kiwi fruit

Green kiwi fruit looks good in fruit **salad**.

Ll   lime

Limes are green and grow
on trees.

Mm   mango
Nn   nectarine

nectarine

stone

mango

Mangoes and nectarines have a **stone** inside them.

Oo   orange

Oranges are juicy!

They have seeds inside them.

Pp   pastry
Qq   quiche

Pastry is the base for a **quiche**.

Rr   red

This red apple is a crunchy food.

Ss   salad

This is a green **salad** made from lettuce.

Tt   tomato

You can put red tomatoes
in your salad.

Uu   under

Radishes grow under the ground.

Vv vegetable

Onions, turnips and potatoes
are **vegetables**.

Ww   white

Rice and cauliflower are
white foods.

Xx

We eat hot cross buns at Easter time.

The cross on the buns looks like the letter X.

Yy yellow
Zz zest

The peel of yellow lemons
is called zest.

Glossary

 **fruit**
the (sweet) part of a plant where
the seeds are

 **honey**
a sweet sticky food made
by bees

 **jam**
a sweet food made from fruit.
It is put on bread.

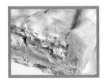 **pastry**
food made of flour, butter and water
as a base for pies and quiche

 **quiche**
a dish with a pastry base and a
filling made with eggs

 **salad**
a cold dish made up of chopped
fruit or vegetables

 **stone**
one hard seed inside a fruit

 **vegetable**
a plant or part of a plant that
can be eaten as a food

23

Index

apples   15

avocados   3

cauliflower   20

dinner   4

fruit   6, 7, 23

grapes   7

honey   8, 23

honeydew melon   6

ice cream   8

jam   9, 23

kiwi fruit   10

lemons   22

lettuces   16

limes   11

mangoes   12

nectarines   12

onions   19

oranges   13

pastry   14, 23

potatoes   19

quiches   14, 23

radishes   18

rice   20

salads   16, 17, 23

star fruit   21

tomatoes   17

turnips   19

vegetables   5, 19, 23

Titles in the Colours We Eat series include:

Hardback   1 844 21605 5

Hardback   1 844 21606 3

Hardback   1 844 21607 1

Hardback   1 844 21608 X

Hardback   1 844 21609 8

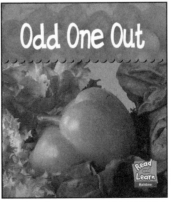

Hardback   1 844 21610 1

Find out about the other titles in this series on our website www.raintreepublishers.co.uk